*Woman's Rights Conventions*

*Seneca Falls & Rochester*

# Woman's Rights Conventions

## Seneca Falls & Rochester

## 1848

*Woman's Rights Convention, Seneca Falls, N.Y., 1848*

**ARNO & THE NEW YORK TIMES**
New York · 1969

# PROCEEDINGS

## OF THE

# WOMAN'S RIGHTS CONVENTIONS,

### HELD AT

## SENECA FALLS & ROCHESTER, N. Y.,

### JULY & AUGUST, 1848.

———•———

NEW YORK:

ROBERT J. JOHNSTON, PRINTER,

No. 59 DUANE STREET.

1870.

# PROCEEDINGS

OF THE

# WOMAN'S RIGHTS CONVENTION,

HELD AT THE

## UNITARIAN CHURCH, ROCHESTER, N. Y.

AUGUST 2, 1848,

*TO CONSIDER THE RIGHTS OF WOMAN, POLITICALLY, RELIGIOUSLY AND INDUSTRIALLY.*

———•———

REVISED BY MRS. AMY POST.

———•———

NEW YORK:

ROBERT J. JOHNSTON, PRINTER,

No. 59 DUANE STREET.

1870.

# REPORT.

A CONVENTION to discuss the SOCIAL, CIVIL, AND RELIGIOUS CONDITION OF WOMAN, was called by the women of Seneca County, N. Y., and held at the village of Seneca Falls, in the Wesleyan Chapel, on the 19th and 20th of July, 1848.

The question was discussed throughout two entire days ; the first day by women exclusively, the second day men participated in the deliberations. LUCRETIA MOTT, of Philadelphia, was the moving spirit of the occasion.

On the morning of the 19th, the Convention assembled at 11 o'clock. The meeting was organized by appointing MARY McCLINTOCK Secretary. The object of the meeting was then stated by ELIZABETH C. STANTON ; after which, remarks were made by LUCRETIA MOTT, urging the women present to throw aside the trammels of education, and not allow their new position to prevent them from joining in the debates of the meeting. The Declaration of Sentiments, offered for the acceptance of the Convention, was then read by E. C. STANTON. A proposition was made to have it re-read by paragraph, and after much consideration, some changes were suggested and adopted. The propriety of obtaining the signatures of men to the Declaration was discussed in an animated manner ; a vote in favor was given ; but concluding that the final decision would be the legitimate business of the next day, it was referred.

Adjourned to half-past two.

## AFTERNOON SESSION.

In the afternoon, the meeting assembled according to adjournment, and was opened by reading the minutes of the morning session. E. C. STANTON then addressed the meeting, and was followed by LUCRETIA MOTT. The reading of the Declaration was called for, an addition having been inserted since the morning session. A vote taken upon

4

the amendment was carried, and papers circulated to obtain signatures. The following resolutions were then read :

Whereas the great precept of nature is conceded to be, " that man shall pursue his own true and substantial happiness." Blackstone, in his Commentaries, remarks, that this law of Nature being coeval with mankind, and dictated by God himself, is of course superior in obligation to any other. It is binding over all the globe, in all countries, and at all times ; no human laws are of any validity if contrary to this, and such of them as are valid, derive all their force, and all their validity, and all their authority, mediately and immediately, from this original; therefore,

Resolved, That such laws as conflict, in any way, with the true and substantial happiness of woman, are contrary to the gr at precept of nature, and of no validity ; for this is " superior in obligation to any other."

Resolved, That all laws which prevent woman from occupying such a station in society as her conscience shall dictate, or which place her in a position inferior to that of man, are contrary to the great precept of nature, and therefore of no force or authority.

Resolved, That woman is man's equal—was intended to be so by the Creator, and the highest good of the race demands that she should be recognized as such.

Resolved, That the women of this country ought to be enlightened in regard to the laws under which they live, that they may no longer publish their degradation, by declaring themselves satisfied with their present position, nor their ignorance, by asserting that they have a'l the rights they want.

Resolved, That inasmuch as man, while claiming for himself intellectual superiority, does not accord to woman moral superiority, it is pre-eminently his duty to encourage her to speak, and teach, as she has an opportunity, in all religious assemblies.

Resolved, That the same amount of virtue, delicacy, and refinement of behavior, that is required of woman in the social state, should also be required of man, and the same transgressions should be visited with equal severity on both man and woman.

Resolved, That the objection of indelicacy and impropriety, which is so often brought against woman when she addresses a public audience, comes with a very ill-grace from those who enccurage, by their attendance, her appearance on the stage, in the concert, or in feats of the circus.

Resolved, That woman has too long rested satisfied in the circumscribed limits which corrupt customs and a perverted application of the Scriptures have marked out for her, and that it is time she should move in the enlarged sphere which her great Creator has assigned her.

Resolved, That it is the duty of the women of this country to secure to themselves their sacred right to the elective franchise.

Resolved, That the equality of human rights results necessarily from the fact of the identity of the race in capabilities and responsibilities.

Resolved, therefore, That, being invested by the Creator with the same capabilities, and the same consciousness of responsibility for their exercise, it is demonstrably the right and duty of woman, equally with man, to promote every righteous cause, by every righteous means ; and especially in regard to the great subjects of morals and religion, it is self-evidently her right to participate with her brother in teaching them, both in private and in public, by writing and by speaking, by any instrumentalities proper to be used, and in any assemblies proper to be held ; and this being a self-evident truth, growing out of the divinely implanted principles of human nature, any custom or authority adverse to it, whether modern or wearing the hoary sanction of antiquity, is to be regarded as a self-evident falsehood, and at war with mankind.

LUCRETIA MOTT read a humorous article from a newspaper, written by MARTHA C. WRIGHT. After an address by E. W. McCLINTOCK, the meeting adjourned to 10 o'clock the next morning.

In the evening, LUCRETIA MOTT spoke with her usual eloquence and power to a large and intelligent audience on the subject of Reform in general.

# THURSDAY MORNING.

The Convention assembled at the hour appointed, JAMES MOTT, of Philadelphia, in the chair. The minutes of the previous day having been read, E. C. STANTON again read the Declaration of Sentiments, which was freely discussed by LUCRETIA MOTT, ANSEL BASCOM, S. E. WOODWORTH, THOMAS and MARY ANN McCLINTOCK, FREDERICK DOUGLASS, AMY POST, CATHARINE STEBBINS and ELIZABETH C. STANTON, and was unanimously adopted, as follows :

## DECLARATION OF SENTIMENTS.

When, in the course of human events, it becomes necessary for one portion of the family of man to assume among the people of the earth a position different from that which they have hitherto occupied, but one to which the laws of nature and of nature's God entitle them, a decent respect to the opinions of mankind requires that they should declare the causes that impel them to such a course.

We hold these truths to be self-evident : that all men and women are created equal; that they are endowed by their Creator with certain inalienable rights, that among these are life, liberty. and the pursuit of happiness ; that to secure these rights governments are instituted, deriving their just powers from the consent of the governed, Whenever any form of government becomes destructive of these ends, it is the right of those who suffer from it to refuse allegiance to it, and to insist upon the institution of a new government, laying its foundation on such principles, and organizing its powers in such form as to them shall seem most likely to effect their safety and happiness. Prudence, indeed, will dictate that governments long established should not be changed for light and transient causes ; and accordingly, all experience hath shown that mankind are more disposed to suffer, while evils are sufferable, than to right themselves by abolishing the forms to which they were accustomed. But when a long train of abuses and usurpations, pursuing invariably the same object evinces a design to reduce them under absolute despotism, it is their duty to throw off such government, and to provide new guards for their future security. Such has been the patient sufferance of the women under this government, and such is now the necessity which constrains them to demand the equal station to which they are entitled.

The history of mankind is a history of repeated injuries and usurpations on the part of man toward woman, having in direct object the establishment of an absolute tyranny over her. To prove this, let facts be submitted to a candid world.

He has never permitted her to exercise her inalienable right to the elective franchise.

He has compelled her to submit to laws, in the formation of which she had no voice.

He has withheld from her rights which are given 'o the most ignorant and degraded men—both natives and foreigners.

Having deprived her of this first right of a citizen, the elective franchise, thereby leaving her without representation in the halls of legislation, he has oppressed her on all sides.

He has made her, if married, in the eye of the law, civilly dead.

He has taken from her all right in property, even to the wages she earns.

He has made her, morally, an irresponsible being, as she can commit many crimes with impunity, provided they be done in the presence of her husband. In the covenant of marriage, she is compelled to promise obedience to her husband, he becoming, to all intents and purposes, her master—the law giving him power to deprive her of her liberty, and to administer chastisement.

He has so framed the laws of divorce, as to what shall be the proper causes of divorce ; in case of separation, to whom the guardianship of the children shall be given ; as to be wholly regardless of the happiness of women—the law, in all cases, going upon a false supposition of the supremacy of man, and giving all power into his hands.

After depriving her of all rights as a married woman, if single and the owner of property, he has taxed her to support a government which recognizes her only when her property can be made profitable to it.

He has monopolized nearly all the profitable employments, and from those she is permitted to follow, she receives but a scanty remuneration.

He closes against her all the avenues to wealth and distinction, which he considers most honorable to himself. As a teacher of theology, medicine, or law, she is not known.

He has denied her the facilities for obtaining a thorough education —all colleges being closed against her.

He allows her in Church, as well as State, but a subordinate position, claiming Apostolic authority for her exclusion from the ministry, and, with some exceptions, from any public participation in the affairs of the Church.

He has created a false public sentiment, by giving to the world a different code of morals for men and women, by which moral delinquencies which exclude women from society, are not only tolerated but deemed of little account in man.

He has usurped the prerogative of Jehovah himself, claiming it as his right to assign for her a sphere of action, when that belongs to her conscience and to her God.

He has endeavored, in every way that he could, to destroy her confidence in her own powers, to lessen her self-respect, and to make her willing to lead a dependent and abject life.

Now, in view of this entire disfranchisement of one-half the people of this country, their social and religious degradation,—in view of the unjust laws above mentioned, and because women do feel themselves aggrieved, oppressed, and fraudulently deprived of their most sacred rights, we insist that they have immediate admission to all the rights and privileges which belong to them as citizens of the United States.

In entering upon the great work before us, we anticipate no small amount of misconception, misrepresentation, and ridicule ; but we shall use every instrumentality within our power to effect our object. We shall employ agents, circulate tracts, petition the state and national legislatures, and endeavor to enlist the pulpit and the press in our behalf. We hope this Convention will be followed by a series of Conventions, embracing every part of the country.

Firmly relying upon the final triumph of the Right and the True, we do this day affix our signatures to this declaration.

| | |
|---|---|
| Lucretia Mott, | Hannah Plant, |
| Harriet Cady Eaton, | Lucy Jones, |
| Margaret Pryor, | Sarah .Whitney, |
| Elizabeth Cady Stanton, | Mary H. Hallowell, |
| Eunice Newton Foote, | Elizabeth Conklin, |
| Mary Ann McClintock, | Sally Pitcher, |
| Margaret Schooley, | Mary Conklin, |
| Martha C. Wright, | Susan Quinn, |
| Jane C. Hunt, | Mary S. Mirror, |
| Amy Post, | Phebe King, |
| Catharine F. Stebbins, | Julia Ann Drake, |
| Mary Ann Frink, | Charlotte Woodward, |
| Lydia Mount, | Martha Underhill, |
| Delia Matthews, | Dorothy Matthews, |
| Catharine C. Paine, | Eunice Barker, |
| Elizabeth W. McClintock, | Sarah R. Woods, |

8

Malvina Seymour,
Phebe Mosher,
Catharine Shaw,
Deborah Scott,
Sarah Hallowell,
Mary McClintock,
Mary Gilbert,
Sophrone Taylor,
Cynthia Davis,
Mary Martin,
P. A. Culvert,
Susan R. Doty,
Rebecca Race,
Sarah A. Mosher,
Mary E. Vail,
Lucy Spalding,
Lavinia Latham,
Sarah Smith,

Lydia Gild,
Sarah Hoffman,
Elizabeth Leslie,
Martha Ridley,
Rachel D. Bonnel,
Betsey Tewksbury,
Rhoda Palmer,
Margaret Jenkins,
Cynthia Fuller,
Eliza Martin,
Maria E. Wilbur,
Elizabeth D. Smith,
Caroline Barker,
Ann Porter,
Experience Gibbs,
Antoinette F. Segur,
Hannah J. Latham,
Sarah Sisson.

The following are the names of the gentlemen present in favor of the movement.

Richard P. Hunt,
Samuel D. Tilman,
Justin Williams,
Elisha Foote,
Frederick Douglass,
Henry W. Seymour,
Henry Seymour,
David Salding,
William G. Barker,
Elias J. Doty,
John Jones,
William S. Dell,
James Mott,
William Burroughs,
Robert Smalldridge,
Jacob Matthews,

Charles L. Hoskins,
Thomas McClintock,
Saron Phillips,
Jacob Chamberlain,
Jonathan Metcalf,
Nathan J. Milliken,
S. E. Woodworth,
Edward F. Underhill,
George W. Pryor,
Joel Bunker,
Isaac Van Tassel,
Thomas Dell,
E. W. Capron,
Stephen Shear,
Henry Hatley,
Azaliah Schooley.

The meeting adjourned until two o'clock.

## AFTERNOON SESSION.

At the appointed hour the meeting convened. The minutes having been read, the resolutions of the day before were read, and taken up separately. Some, from their self-evident truth, elicited but little remark ; others, after some criticism, much debate, and some slight alterations, were finally passed by a large majority. The meeting closed by a forcible speech from LUCRETIA MOTT.

Adjourned to half-past seven o'clock.

# EVENING SESSION.

The meeting opened by reading the minutes, THOMAS McCLINTOCK in the chair. As there had been no opposition expressed during the Convention to this movement, and although, after repeated invitations no objections had presented themselves, E. C. STANTON volunteered an address in defence of the many severe accusations brought against the much-abused "Lords of Creation."

THOMAS McCLINTOCK then read several extracts from Blackstone, in proof of woman's servitude to man; after which LUCRETIA MOTT offered and spoke to the following resolution :

Resolved, That the speedy success of our cause depends upon the zealous and untiring efforts of both men and women, for the overthrow of the monopoly of the pulpit, and for the securing to woman an equal participation with men in the various trades, professions and commerce.

The resolution was adopted.

M. A. McCLINTOCK, JR., delivered a short, but impressive, address calling upon woman to arouse from her lethargy and be true to herself and her God. When she had concluded, FREDERICK DOUGLASS arose, and in an excellent and appropriate speech, ably supported the cause of woman.

The meeting was closed by one of LUCRETIA MOTT's most beautiful and spiritual appeals. She commanded the earnest attention of that large audience for nearly an hour.

M. A. McCLINTOCK, E. N. FOOTE, AMY POST, E. W. McCLINTOCK, and E. C. STANTON were appointed a committee to prepare the proceedings of the Convention for publication.

# REPORT

# WOMAN'S RIGHTS CONVENTION,

HELD AT

## Seneca Falls, N. Y.,

JULY 19TH & 20TH, 1848.

———◆———

### ROCHESTER:
PRINTED BY JOHN DICK,
AT THE NORTH STAR OFFICE.
1848.

# REPORT

At an early hour the church was well filled.

Amy Post called the meeting to order and stated that at a preliminary meeting, held the previous evening at Protection Hall, herself, Sarah D. Fish and Rhoda De Garmo, were appointed a Committee to Nominate Officers for this Convention, and that they had concluded to propose the following names : *President*—Abigail Bush ; *Vice-President*—Laura Murray ; *Secretaries*—Elizabeth McClintock, Sarah L. Hallowell and Catharine A. F. Stebbins.

The report of the committee was unanimously adopted by the Convention, excepting the case of Elizabeth McClintock, who declined accepting the office, on the ground of being unprepared to have a woman the presiding officer, therefore, she proposed the name of Mary H. Hallowell in her place, which being seconded by Mary Ann McClintock, she was duly appointed. To our great surprise, two or three other women—glorious reformers, well deserving the name—coming from a distance to attend the meeting, at first refused to take their seats upon the platform, or otherwise co-operate with the Convention, for the same cause. But as the meeting proceeded, and they had listened to some opening remarks from our gentle but heroic President, their fears for the honor of the Convention subsided, after which they worked nobly for the cause that had called us together, and the meeting proceeded harmoniously to the end.

Prayer was offered by Rev. Mr. Wicher.

The minutes of the preliminary meeting were then read by Sarah L. Hallowell, at which time much anxiety was manifested concerning the low voices of the women, and whenever reading or speaking was attempted, without giving time for adapting the voice to the size of the house, cries of "louder," "louder," nearly drowned every other sound, when the President arose and said :

4

"Friends, we present ourselves here before you, as an oppressed class, with trembling frames and faltering tongues, and we do not expect to be able to speak so as to be heard by all at first, but we trust we shall have the sympathy of the audience, and that you will bear with our weakness, now in the infancy of the movement. Our trust in the omnipotency of right is our only faith that we shall succeed."

WILLIAM C. NELL then read an eloquent address, highly commendatory of the energies and rare devotion of woman in every good cause, illustrated by facts in proof of her equality with man ; adding that he should never cease to award the grateful homage of his heart for their zeal in behalf of the oppressed class with which he stood identified.

LUCRETIA MOTT arose and said, that although she was grateful for the eloquent speech just given, she must be allowed to object to some portions of it ; such as styling "woman the better half of creation, and man a tyrant." Man had become so accustomed to speak of woman in the language of flattering compliments, that he indulges in such expressions unawares. She said that man was not a tyrant by nature, but had been made tyrannical by the power which had, by general consent, been conferred upon him ; she merely wished that woman might be entitled to equal rights, and *acknowledged* as the equal of man, not his superior. Woman is equally tyrannical when she has irresponsible power, and we shall never place her in a true position, until we have formed a just estimate of mankind as created by God. She thought there were some evidences of improvement —instanced the reform in the literature of the day, the sickly sentimentality of the "Ladies Department," which was fast disappearing, perceiving that the mind requires more substantial food.

WM. C. NELL disclaimed all intention of flattery; he did not think *that* flattery which was spoken in truth.

A letter was read from GERRIT SMITH, approving cordially of the object of the Convention, and expressed his deep regret in not being able to be present.

ELIZABETH CADY STANTON then read the Declaration of Rights, which had been adopted by the Woman's Rights Convention held at Seneca Falls, which was cordially adopted by the meeting.

An expression of sentiment upon this Declaration of Rights being invited by the President, Mrs. Stanton expressed a hope that the invitation would be accepted. That if there were any present who did not agree with them in their notions of the Rights of Woman, that they would then and there make their objections, and not, as at Seneca Falls, keep silent through all our deliberations, and afterwards, on the Sabbath day, use the pulpit throughout the town to denounce them, where they could not, of course, be allowed to reply.

Hereupon a Mr. COLTON, of Connecticut, spoke freely of his great interest in the cause of woman. He loved the ladies as well as they loved themselves, but he would not have woman excel her proper sphere. He thought her place was at home, instead of engaging in the strife and contention of the political world. Home was her empire and her throne, and he should deprecate exceedingly her occupying the pulpit.

LUCRETIA MOTT replied in a speech of great sarcasm and eloquence. She said that the gentleman from New Haven had objected to woman occupying the pulpit, and indeed she could scarcely see how any one educated in New Haven, Ct., could think otherwise than he did. She said, we had all got our notions too much from the clergy, instead of the Bible. The Bible, she contended, had none of the prohibitions in regard to woman ; and spoke of the "honorable women, not a few," etc., and desired Mr. Colton to read his Bible over again, and see if there was anything there to prohibit woman from being a religious teacher.

She then complimented the members of that church for opening their doors to a Woman's Rights Convention, and said that a few years ago, the Female Moral Reform Society of Philadelphia applied for the use of a church in that city in which to hold one of their meetings ; they were only allowed the use of the basement, and on condition that none of the women should speak at the meeting. Accordingly a D.D. was called upon to preside, and another to read the ladies report of the Society.

Hon. WILLIAM C. BLOSS next spoke. He seemed disposed to allow all the privileges asked for by the women, except the elective franchise, and even that he almost admitted that good would result from ; but he portrayed many obstacles in the path of that reform. He inquired if there was not a natural disqualification ? did not boys and girls exhibit dissimilar taste in the choice of playthings ? the one preferring the noisy hammer, or the hoop, while the other, the darling doll at home ? and were not these same traits carried out and more fully developed in after life ? and he doubted if the ladies would use the right, if it were conferred upon them.

MILO D. CODDING also objected to that part of the Declaration which advocated woman's right to the elective franchise. He thought it sufficient for woman to vote through her father, brothers, or husband, but he finally concluded by wishing her a hearty God speed in her enterprise.

FREDERICK DOUGLASS followed in an eloquent and argumentative appeal for Woman's Rights, replying in a clear and conclusive manner to the gentleman who had spoken on the other side. He thought that the true basis of rights was the capacity of individuals ; and as for himself, he should not dare claim a right that he would not concede to woman. As to the enfranchisement of woman, it need not be questioned whether she would use that right or not ; man had no right to withhold it from her.

He alluded to the oppressive customs of the Old World, which so wronged woman; subjecting her to the most laborious, as well as degrading, means for a livelihood, which he had beheld with his own eyes. He would see woman elevated to an equal position with man in every relation of life.

At the close of Frederick Douglass's speech, a young bride, REBECCA M. SANDFORD, came forward to the altar and asked the privilege of saying a few words. She said she was on her way westward, but hearing of this Convention, she had waited over one train to add her mite in favor of the demand now made by the true women of this day and generation. She eloquently advocated the just claims of woman to an entire equality with man. Her remarks were listened to with close attention, and produced a marked impression upon the audience, furnishing an evidence, if any were still needed, that Woman's voice and ability could effect much in the sacred desk (so-called), in legislative halls, or anywhere where true eloquence is required.

Her husband, who accompanied her, remained standing near her (with respectful silence) while she spoke as follows :

It is with diffidence that I speak upon the deliberations before us, not a diffidence resulting from any doubt of the worthiness of the cause, but from the fear that its *depth* and *power* can be but meagrely portrayed by me.

Woman's rights—her civil rights—equal with man's—not an equality of moral and religious influence, for who dare to deny her that ? but an equality of exertion, and a right to use all the sources of erudition within the reach of man, to build unto herself a name for her talents, energy and integrity. We do not positively say that our intellect is as capable as man's to assume, and at once to hold, these rights, or that our hearts are as willing to enter into his actions ; for if we did not believe it, we would not contend for them, and if men did not believe it, they would not withhold them with a smothered silence. From Semiramis to Victoria we have found the Women of History equal to the emergencies before them ! and more than equal—their perceptions accurately measuring the consequences of the future by the influences of the present ; their judgment, their elevation and their will, using their prerogatives to change and improve their epoch ! The world has seen woman in power ; and the after history of that age tells of the abuse of power.

But I do not intend to speak of oppressive and tyrannical *power* as woman's *right*, but that if you will galvanize her into civil liberty, you will find her capable of being in it, and of sustaining it. Place her in equal power, and you will find her capable of not abusing it ! Give her the elective franchise, and there will be an unseen, yet a deep and universal movement of the people to elect into office only those who are pure in intention and honest in sentiment ! Give her the privilege to co-operate in making the laws she submits to, and there will be harmony without severity, and justice without oppression. Make her, if married, a *living being* in the eye of the law—she will not assume beyond duty ; give her right of property, and y ou may justly tax her patrimony as the result of her wages. Open to her your colleges—your legislative, your municipal, your domestic laws may be purified and ennobled. *Forbid her not*, and she will use moderation.

These thoughts of right and liberty are young with us. The American Independence was once young ; and to what has it now progressed ? The draft of *our* Declaration may, in some respects, be faulty and feeble. So may have been the first draft of the Constitution of the United States. But what right has it not protected, what grievance not redressed, and what exertions not encouraged ?

Is it not well for us, upon the excitement of this sympathetic movement, to steadily consider some one great aim of lasting good ? Perhaps we are called upon by Providence, through these all-stirring inspirations of rights, to finish the work so nobly commenced by man —to wipe from our national escutcheon that spot—*slavery*. Perhaps it is for us to say to the slave on American soil : you are an American ! therefore free. Perhaps it is for us to bless, protect and elevate the people. The consummation of our exertions will note a procession like that of yesterday,* beneath the banners of liberty, faith, and hope, with happiness and gratitude in every heart, parading the streets of every city from Washington to New Orleans. If so, let us nerve to the struggle ! Let us, by convention and combination, assert, contend for, and secure our rights—and then, by prudence and energy, merit the blessing of saying to master and slave, Creation is Abolition.

Here will be one effect, perhaps unlooked for, if we are raised to equal administration with man. It will classify intellect. The heterogeneous triflings which now, I am very sorry to say, occupy so much of our time, will be neglected ; fashion's votaries will silently fall off ; dishonest exertions for rank in society will be scorned ; extravagance in toilet will be detested ; that meagre and worthless pride of station will be forgotten ; the honest earnings of dependents will be paid ; popular demagogues crushed ; imposters unpatronized ; true genius

* The Celebration of Emancipation in the West Indies.

sincerely encouraged ; and, above all, pawned integrity redeemed.
And why ? Because enfranchised woman then will feel the burthens
of her responsibilities, and can strive for elevation, and will reach all
knowledge within her grasp.

If all this is accomplished, man need not fear pomposity, fickleness,
or an unhealthy enthusiasm at his dear fireside ; we can be as dutiful,
submissive, endearing as daughters, wives and mothers, even if we
hang the wreath of domestic harmony upon the eagle's talons.

Mrs. Sandford was followed by ANN EDGEWORTH who spoke in a
feeling and happy manner at some length.

The meeting then adjourned until half-past two.

## AFTERNOON SESSION.

At the hour appointed, the house was well filled with an intelligent and inquiring audience. President in the chair.

An opportunity for prayer was given ; none being offered, the PRESI-
DENT informed the meeting that a letter had been received from
JAMES C. JACKSON, approving the object of the Convention, and it
was decided to make the reading of the letter the first business of the
present session. We regret that the letter has been lost, and cannot
be laid before our readers.

SARAH C. OWEN next read an address, earnestly portraying many of
the wrongs and outrages to which woman is subjected, an extract of
which follows :

### ADDRESS OF SARAH C. OWEN.

The embarrassment under which we labor in presenting our views
of the subject upon which we are convened, cannot be estimated ;
naught but a sense of duty could have nerved us to this work. Bona-
parte, when remonstrated with by one of his ablest Generals, against
some of his daring attempts, replied, "The word *impossible* is not in
the French language," and we now claim he right of erasing it from
our vocabulary, so far as it precludes our efforts in the cause of Equal
Rights.

It is a generally received truth, that the proper study of mankind
is *man ;* virtually denying that *woman* is included in the intelligent
part of creation ; that she is endowed with mental powers that could
be properly extended beyond the narrow bounds of the domestic
circle. We have possessed our souls in all possible patience, waiting
for some day-star of hope and promise to beam upon our pathway,
assuring us that he who had robbed us would restore without this indi-
vidual effort ; but patience has expired, and hope fled ; therefore we
now raise the banner of Equal Rights, with the assurance that patience

and perseverance is the secret of success in all crusades against oppression and wrong.

We hear the cry, "Who hath, or wherein have we robbed thee?" I assert that woman is robbed of all those inalienable rights which man enjoys, those which our Creator never thus unequally assigned to his children. And it needs no particular demonstration to prove that the disparity of intellect depends in no way on physical strength and stature ; this idea has its origin in the bias of a wrong education, saying nothing of selfishness.

It has been reiterated from time immemorial that woman is the weaker vessel, that she was designed to occupy a lower sphere than man, to be subject to all the restraints he deems proper.

Rosseau says that woman ought to have but little liberty ; that she is apt to indulge herself excessively in what is allowed her ; and thus every aspiration after knowledge is checked. If she should perchance wish to know anything, she must ask her husband at home. She is as nearly circumscribed as was he who went to confession and said he had been *thinking*, when the priest angrily interrupted him by asking what business *he* had to *think;* but woman may think provided she thinks with her husband. No doubt, many, if accused of this tyranny, would reply, "Is thy servant a dog that he should thus wrong one whom he has vowed to protect?" but this was applied to her person, not her opinions, or what she considered her rights.

Observe the difference, when, after marriage, she assumes her right to dispose of, as she sees fit, the product of her own hard-earned toil, to which, by law, she has no right nor title, except the right of dower. She contends on the ground of righteousness, while he withholds on the false ground of legality. Should she, following his example, contend earnestly for her rights, anarchy and confusion ensue, then he is reminded of the *wise* provision of law ; his right to whip her, provided he confines himself to a stick not larger than his thumb. No wonder Elizabeth rejected the most powerful Princes of Europe, fearing the power of an usurper. She declared to her Parliament that the epitaph which would best please her, would be, "*Here lies a Virgin Queen !*" We have every day examples of the Chalmucks, who marry for only one year.

In this christian land, in this day of intelligence, we are far behind those of heathen lands in centuries past, woman is considered of less value than the most abject slave. By law, five slaves in the scale of political power numbers the same as three white men, while one million of white women weigh just nothing at all.

We ask our friends if any logical reason can be assigned why woman should not be as well educated as man ? The same facilities afforded her for the development of her intellectual powers would gather in a vast waste of intelligence, which has been lost to the world for want of encouragement.

An experienced cashier of this city remarked to me that women might be as good book-keepers as men ; but men have monopolized every lucrative situation, from the dry-goods merchant down to whitewashing. Who does not feel, as she sees a stout, athletic man standing behind the counter measuring lace, ribbons and tape, that he is monopolizing a woman's place, while thousands of rich acres in our western world await his coming. This year, a woman, for the first time, has taken her place in one of our regular medical colleges. We rejoice to hear that by her dignity of manner, application to study, and devotion to the several branches of the profession she has chosen, she has secured the respect of her professors and class, and reflected lasting honor upon her whole sex. Thus we hail in Elizabeth Blackwell a pioneer for woman in this profession.

It is by this inverted order of society that woman is obliged to ply the needle by day and by night, to procure even a scanty pittance for her dependent family. Let men become producers, as nature has designed them, and women be educated to fill all those stations which require less physical strength, and we should soon modify many of our social evils. I am informed by the seamstresses of this city that they get but thirty cents for making a satin vest, and from twelve to thirty for making pants, and coats in the same proportion. Man has such a contemptible idea of woman, that he thinks she cannot even sew as well as a man, and he often goes to a *tailor*, and pays him double and even thriple for making a suit, when it merely passes through his hands, after a woman has made every stitch of it so neatly that he discovers no difference. Who does not see gross injustice in this inequality of wages and violation of rights ? To prove that woman is capable of prosecuting the mercantile business, we have a noble example in this city in Mrs. Gifford, who has sustained herself with credit. She has bravely triumphed over all obloquy and discouragement attendant on such a novel experiment, and made for herself an independent living.

In the fields of benevolence, woman has done great and noble works for the safety and stability of the nation. Now, when man shall see the wisdom of recognizing a coworker in her, then may be looked for the dawning of a perfect day, when woman shall stand where God designed she should—on an even platform with man himself.

Sarah D. Fish also eloquently set forth some of the causes of woman's degradation, and urged her entreatingly to come forward to the work of elevation.

Several resolutions were then read, which were presented by Amy Post to the preliminary meeting, and referred to this without discussion. LUCRETIA MOTT ably advocated them, though she pronounced them too tame ; she wished to have something more stirring.

Mrs. ROBERTS, who had been requested to investigate the wrongs of the laboring classes, and to invite that oppressed portion of the community to attend the Convention, and take part in its delibera- tions, made some appropriate remarks relative to the intolerable servi- tude and small remuneration paid to the working class of women. She reported the average price of labor for seamstresses to be from 31 to 38 cents a day, and board from $1.25 to $1.50 per week to be de- ducted therefrom, and they were generally obliged to take half or more in due bills, which were payable in goods at certain stores, thereby obliging them many times to pay extortionate prices, etc.

Mrs. GALLOY corrobated the statement, having herself experienced some of the oppressions of this portion of our citizens, and expressed her gratitude that the subject was claiming the attention of this benevolent and intelligent class of community.

Mrs. E. C. STANTON offered a resolution respecting the wages of house servants, which she thought quite too low for the labor they performed, and urged the necessity of reformers commencing at home.

Mrs. MOTT remarked that our aim should be to elevate the lowly and aid the weak. She compared the condition of woman to that of the free colored population, and dwelt upon the progress *they* had made within the last few years, urging woman to imitate them in their perseverance through oppression and prejudice, and said, " while wo- man is regarded as an inferior being, while the Bible is brought for- ward to prove the right of her present position, and while she is dis- posed to feel satisfied with it, all these efforts can do but little. We cannot expect to do much by meeting in Conventions for those borne down by the oppressor, unless the oppressed themselves *feel* and *act,* and while so little attention is paid to her education, and so little respect for woman. She spoke of the contrast in the education of boys and girls in England. The common school there for boys show improvement; mathematics, and many of the higher branches are being taught ; while girls are taught little more than to read and write, and keep their little accounts, sewing being the principle object of at- tention. The teacher told her it would not do to educate them, for the reason that it would unfit them for servants.

She said that she would grant that woman's intellect may be feeble, because she had been so long crushed ; but is that any reason why she should be deprived of her equal rights ? Does one man have fewer rights than another because his intellect is inferior ? If not, why should woman ? Let woman arise and demand her rights, and in a few years we shall see a different mental development. She regarded this as the beginning of the day when woman shall rise and occupy her appropriate position in society.

Many pertinent remarks were made upon the legal and social inequality of woman by ANN EDGWORTH, RHODA DE GARMO, E. C. STANTON, Mrs. ROBERTS, and others.

ELIZABETH McCLINTOCK read some notes, taken from a sermon preached at Seneca Falls, on the Sunday following the Woman's Rights Convention held there, reviewing their Declaration of Sentiments, to which E. C. Stanton had published an able reply. At the request of Lucretia Mott, she also read, in an admirable manner, the following spirited piece of poetry, written by MARIA W. CHAPMAN, in reply to a pastoral letter, signed "Lords of Creation."

### "THE TIMES THAT TRY MEN'S SOULS."

#### (LANGUAGE OF THE RESOLUTION.)

CONFUSION has seized us, and all things go wrong,
The women have leaped from "their spheres,"
And, instead of fixed stars, shoot as comets along,
And are setting the world by the ears!
In courses erratic they're wheeling through space,
In brainless confusion and meaningless chase.

In vain do our knowing ones try to compute
Their return to the orbit designed;
They're glanced at a moment, then onward they shoot,
And are neither "to hold nor to bind;"
So freely they move in their chosen ellipse,
The "Lords of Creation" do fear an eclipse.

They've taken a notion to speak for themselves,
And are wielding the tongue and the pen;
They've mounted the rostrum; the termagant elves,
And—oh horrid!—are talking to men!
With faces unblanched in our presence they come
To harangue us, they say, in behalf of the dumb.

They insist on their right to petition and pray,
That St. Paul, in Corinthians, has given them rules
For appearing in public; despite what those say
Whom we've trained to instruct them in schools;
But vain such instructions, if women may scan
And quote texts of Scripture to favor their plan.

Our grandmother's learning consisted of yore,
In spreading their generous boards;
In twisting the distaff, or mopping the floor,
And *obeying the will of their Lords.*
Now, misses may reason, and think, and debate,
Till unquestioned submission is quite out of date.

Our clergy have preached on the sin and the shame
  Of woman, when out of " her sphere,"
And labored *divinely* to ruin her fame,
  And shorten this horrid career,
But for spiritual guidance no longer they look
To Fulsom, or Winslow, or learned Parson Cook.

Our wise men have tried to exorcise in vain—
  The turbulent spirits abroad :
As well might we deal with the fetterless main,
  Or conquer ethereal essence with sword,
Like the devils of Milton, they rise from each blow,
With spirit unbroken, insulting the foe.

Our patriot fathers, of eloquent fame,
  Waged war against tangible forms ;
Aye, *their* foes were men—and if ours were the same,
  *We* might speedily quiet their storms,
But ah! their descendants enjoy not such bliss—
The assumptions of Britain were nothing to this.

Could we but array all our force in the field,
  We'd teach these usurpers of power,
That their bodily safety demands they should yield,
  And in presence of manhood should cower ;
But, alas! for our tethered and impotent state,
Chained by notions of knighthood—we can but debate.

Oh! shade of the prophet Mahomet, arise!
  Place woman again in " her sphere,"
And teach that her soul was not born for the skies,
  But to flutter a brief moment here.
This doctrine of Jesus, as preached up by Paul,
If embraced in its spirit, will ruin us all.

LORDS OF CREATION.

The Convention then adjourned until seven o'clock in the evening.

# EVENING SESSION.

PRESIDENT in the Chair. A large and crowded audience still in attendance.

On motion, the Declaration of Sentiments was again read, and one hundred and seven signatures obtained, when another discussion ensued upon the dangerous doctrines.

Mr. SULLEY wished to ask fathers, if they had duly considered this subject, which the women had called a Convention to discuss ? Did they understand what effect this equality would have upon families ? If the husband and wife should differ in politics, or the education of children, how deplorable must be the consequences ?

LUCRETIA MOTT replied by asking the question which is preferable, *ignorant* or *intelligent* differences ?

Mr. SULLEY further asked, when the two heads disagree, who must decide ? There is no Lord Chancellor to whom to apply, and does not St. Paul strictly enjoin obedience to husbands, and that man shall be head of the woman ?

Our ever-able LUCRETIA MOTT replied that in an extensive acquaintance in the Society of Friends, she had never known any difficulty to arise on account of the wife's not having promised *obedience* in the marriage contract. She had never known any other mode of decision, except a resort to argument, and an appeal to reason ; and although in some of the meetings of this Society, women are placed on an equality, none of the results so much dreaded had occurred. She said that many of the opposers of Woman's Rights, who bid us to obey the bachelor, St. Paul, themselves reject his counsel—he advised them not to marry. In general answer, she would quote, "One is your master, even Christ." Although Paul enjoins silence on women in the church, yet he gives directions how they should appear when publicly speaking, and we have scriptural accounts of honorable women not a few, who were religious teachers : *viz.;* Phebe, Priscilla, Tryphena, Triphosa, and the four daughters of Phillip, and various others.

Mrs. STANTON thought the gentleman might be easily answered ; saying that the strongest will, or the superior intellect, now governs the household, as it will in the new order ; she knew many a woman who, to all intents and purposes, is at the head of her family.

Mr. PICKARD asked who, after marriage, should hold the property, and whose name should be retained ? He thought an umpire necessary. He did not see but all business must cease until the consent of both parties be obtained. He saw an impossibility of introducing such rules into society. The gospel had established the unity and oneness of the married pair, etc., etc.

Mrs. STANTON said she thought the gospel, rightly understood, pointed to a oneness of equality, not subordination, and that property should be jointly held. She could see no reason why marriage by false creeds should be made a degradation to woman ; and as to the name ; the custom of taking the husband's name is not universal. When a man has a bad name, in any sense, he might be the gainer by burying himself under the good name of his wife. This last Winter a Mr. Cruikshanks applied to our legistature to have his name changed. Now if he had taken his wife's name in the beginning, he might have saved the legislature the trouble of considering the propriety of releasing the man from such a burthen, to be entailed on the third and fourth generation.

The following resolutions, which had been separately discussed, were again read. AMY POST moved their adoption by the meeting, which was carried with but two or three dissenting voices :

1. Resolved, That we petition our State Legislature for our right to the elective franchise, every year, until our prayer be granted.

2. Resolved, That it is an admitted principle of the American Republic, that the only just power of the Government is derived from the consent of the governed ; and that taxation and representation are inseperable ; and therefore, woman being taxed equally with man, ought not to be deprived of an equal representation in the government.

3. Resolved, That we deplore the apathy and indifference of woman in regard to her rights, thus restricting her to an inferior position in social, religious, and political life, and we urge her to claim an equal right to act on all subjects that interest the human family.

4. Resolved, That the assumption of law to settle estates of men who die without wills, having widows, is an insult to woman, and ought to be regarded as such by every lover of right and equality.

5. Whereas, The husband has the legal right to hire out his wife to service, collect her wages and appropriate it to his own exclusive and independent benefit ; and, whereas, this has contributed to establish that hideous custom, the promise of obedience in the marriage contract, effectually, though insidiously, reducing her almost to the condition of a *slave*, whatever freedom she may have in these respects, being granted as a privilege, not as a right, therefore,

Resolved, That we will seek the overthrow of this barbarous and unrighteous law ; and conjure women no longer to promise obedience in the marriage covenant.

Resolved, That the universal doctrine of the inferiority of woman has ever caused her to distrust her own powers, and paralized her energies, and placed her in that degraded position from which the most strenuous and unremitting effort can alone redeem her. Only by faithful perseverance in the practical exercise of those talents, so long "wrapped in a napkin and buried under the earth," she will regain her long-lost equality with man.

Resolved, That in the persevering and independent course of Miss Blackwell, who recently attended a series of medical lectures in Geneva, and has now gone to Europe to graduate as a physician, we see a harbinger of the day when woman shall stand forth "redeemed and disenthralled," and perform those important duties which are so truly within her sphere.

Resolved, That those who believe the laboring classes of women are oppressed ought to do all in their power to raise their wages, beginning with their own household servants.

Resolved, That it is the duty of woman, whatever her complexion, to assume, as soon as possible, her true position of equality in the social circle, the church, and the state.

Resolved, That we tender our grateful acknowledgment to the Trustees of the Unitarian Church, who have kindly opened their doors for the use of this Convention.

Resolved, That we, the friends who are interested in this cause, gratefully accept the kind offer from the Trustees of the use of Protection Hall, to hold our meetings whenever we wish.

With hearts overflowing with grateful joy, the meeting adjourned *sine die.*

ABIGAIL BUSH, President.

LAURA MURRAY, Vice-Pres.

SARAH L. HALLOWELL,    &#125;
CATHARINE A. F. STEBBINS,  &#125; Secretaries.
MARY H. HALLOWELL,    &#125;